D1738588

NS ALIVE

Sea Lions

by Colleen Sexton

BELLWETHER MEDIA • MINNEAPOLIS, MN

Note to Librarians, Teachers, and Parents:

Blastoff! Readers are carefully developed by literacy experts and combine standards-based content with developmentally appropriate text.

Level 1 provides the most support through repetition of high-frequency words, light text, predictable sentence patterns, and strong visual support.

Level 2 offers early readers a bit more challenge through varied simple sentences, increased text load, and less repetition of high-frequency words.

Level 3 advances early-fluent readers toward fluency through increased text and concept load, less reliance on visuals, longer sentences, and more literary language.

Level 4 builds reading stamina by providing more text per page, increased use of punctuation, greater variation in sentence patterns, and increasingly challenging vocabulary.

Level 5 encourages children to move from "learning to read" to "reading to learn" by providing even more text, varied writing styles, and less familiar topics.

Whichever book is right for your reader, Blastoff! Readers are the perfect books to build confidence and encourage a love of reading that will last a lifetime!

This edition first published in 2008 by Bellwether Media.

No part of this publication may be reproduced in whole or in part without written permission of the publisher. For information regarding permission, write to Bellwether Media Inc., Attention: Permissions Department, Post Office Box 19349, Minneapolis, MN 55419.

Library of Congress Cataloging-in-Publication Data
Sexton, Colleen A., 1967–
  Sea lions / by Colleen Sexton.
    p. cm. – (Blastoff! readers: Oceans alive)
Summary: "Simple text and full color photographs introduce beginning readers to sea lions. Developed by literacy experts for students in kindergarten through third grade"–Provided by publisher.
  Includes bibliographical references and index.
  ISBN-13: 978-1-60014-174-4 (hardcover : alk. paper)
  ISBN-10: 1-60014-174-9 (hardcover : alk. paper)
  1. Sea lions–Juvenile literature. I. Title.

  QL737.P63.S46 2008
  599.79'75–dc22   2007040279

Contents

Sea lions live on the coast of
the **Pacific Ocean**.

4

They live in both cold places
and warm places.

Brown fur covers a sea
lion's long body.

Sea lions have fat called **blubber**. It keeps them warm in cold water.

Male sea lions are much larger than female sea lions. They can be as big as a small car.

Sea lions have round eyes, small ears, and thick **whiskers**.

Sea lions find food in the water. They eat fish, octopuses, crabs, and even penguins.

10

Sea lions can also use their whiskers to feel for food on the ocean floor.

Sea lions can **dive** deep into the ocean to find food.

Most dives last three to nine minutes. Then sea lions come up for air.

Sometimes sea lions are food for other animals. Sharks and killer whales hunt sea lions.

Sea lions swim fast to escape **predators**. They leap in and out of the water to gain speed.

15

front flippers

Sea lions use their front **flippers** to push themselves forward.

They use their back flippers
to change direction.

Sea lions can walk on land. They turn their flippers to the side to walk on them.

Sea lions can move fast over sand and rocks. They can even climb cliffs!

Sea lions live together in a **colony**. They bark, honk, and roar to each other.

They move close together
when they sleep. Sleep
well sea lions!

Glossary

blubber—a thick layer of fat just under the skin; blubber keeps sea lions warm in cold water.

colony—a large group of animals that lives together

dive—to move headfirst in or into the water; sea lions dive deeply and some can hold their breath for up to 40 minutes.

flipper—a wide, flat limb that some ocean animals use to swim

Pacific Ocean—the ocean to the west of the United States

predator—an animal that hunts other animals for food

whiskers—stiff hairs that grow near an animal's mouth; sea lions can use their whiskers to feel their surroundings.

To Learn More

AT THE LIBRARY

Kalman, Bobbie. *Seals and Sea Lions*. New York: Crabtree, 2006.

Lamm, C. Drew. *Sea Lion Roars*. Norwalk, Conn.: Soundprints, 1997.

Staub, Frank J. *Sea Lions*. Minneapolis, Minn.: Lerner, 2000.

Whitehouse, Patricia. *Sea Lion*. Chicago, Ill.: Heinemann, 2003.

ON THE WEB

Learning more about sea lions is as easy as 1, 2, 3.

1. Go to www.factsurfer.com

2. Enter "sea lions" into search box.

3. Click the "Surf" button and you will see a list of related web sites.

With factsurfer.com, finding more information is just a click away.

Index

The images in this book are reproduced through the courtesy of: Dewayne Flowers, front cover; Piumatti Sergio/Age fotostock, pp. 4-5; Tui De Roy/Getty Images, pp. 6-7; Tim Zurowski, pp. 8-9; Chris A Crumley/Alamy, p. 10; Brandon Cole/Getty Images, p. 11; Chris Newbert/Getty Images, pp. 12-13; Fabrice Bettex/Alamy, p. 14; Stuart Westmorland/Getty Images, p. 15; Peter Scoones/Getty Images, p. 16; Stephen Frink/Getty Images, p. 17; Konrad Wothe/Getty Images, pp. 18-19; Michael Nolan/age fotostock, p. 20; Wolfgang Kaehler/Alamy. p. 21.